Today, open your eyes of faith and see the good things God has store for your future.

Faith

Over

Fear

Inspired By:

Tristan Jackson, B.B.A., M.P.A

Dreams bigger than doubts!

Faith stronger than fears!

"Now faith is the substance of things hoped for, the evidence of things not seen."

~Hebrews 11:1~

Text Copyright * 2019

by T. Jackson

Published by T. Jackson
Houston, TX

Printed in the
United States of America

"Blessed is the man who trusts in the Lord and has made the Lord his hope and confidence."

~Jeremiah 17:7

Table of Contents

Author's Note:10

Ch.1:Pursue Your Dreams:13

Ch.2:The Power Of Faith:20

Ch.3:Dreams Bigger Than Fear:26

Ch.4:Fear Will Not Win:32

Ch.5:Greatness:37

Ch.6:Believe It's Possible:44

Ch.7:Shift Your Mindset:52

Ch.8:The Journey:58

Ch.9:Never Give Up:64

Ch.10:Inspiration:73

***Feed your faith and
your fears will starve to death.
~ Author Unknown~***

AUTHOR'S NOTE:

At the heart of this book is the message to never give up on your dreams. My wish in writing faith over fear is that you will be moved and motivated to walk in faith and not fear.

    Choose to believe today.

    Tristan Jackson

Today, I want to declare words of blessings over you. I want to call forth your seeds of greatness. Someone may have told you what can't become, but I'm here to tell you what you can become. You are loved. You are a person of destiny. No weapon formed against you will prosper.

Every morning you are handed 24 golden hours. They are one of the few things in this world that you get free of charge. If you had all the money in the world, you couldn't buy an extra hour. What will you do with this priceless treasure?

~ Author Unknown~

Chapter 1.
Pursue Your Dreams

I am no stranger or casual observer to fear. I have personally felt its powerful grip on my life. But also, I have experienced a peace, trust and faith in God will make a way.

I don't know what you're facing today, but I pray you can lean on your faith. Nothing can defeat our God who cares deeply about you. He will never leave you alone; He will be with you wherever you go. No matter how dark it gets.

Wanting to go to college, I remember like it was yesterday, telling my mom, "Save your money because I am going to college."

My mom would look at me with an expression of defeat on her face because she was barely making it from paycheck to paycheck. Since my parents never had the opportunity to attend college, I was determined to be different.

I wasn't spoiled as a kid growing up at all, living in a single-parent home where having money was a problem. I would see my mother struggle, working hard trying to make ends meet. My daddy would provide as needed. It was taught to me that if you wanted something, you had to figure out a way to get it and then execute that plan.

After graduating from Lamar University with a B.B.A. (Human Resource Management) (2009) and Master in Public Administration (2013).

In 2014, I decided to move back to Houston, Texas. In that same year, God gave me the vision to start my own business—Divine Gift Baskets. YES, I was ready, but thought to myself, "God, a business?" With no road map on how to start a business, I thought immediately that my family, friends, social media connections, and co-workers would buy all of my baskets. Well, I was wrong and was heartbroken.

In 2015, through the power of social media, I contacted an individual that helped me release my first book entitled Dream the Impossible. I had written the book in 2012, and often shopped my book to different publishing companies. It would cost me thousands of dollars to publish. God blessed me with a company that now publishes my books at a reasonable cost. Yes, as a new author, I thought once again that my immediate family, friends, social media contacts, and coworkers would buy all of my books.

Well, I was once again wrong and felt defeated, with the desire to share my story. I have sold over 250 copies of Dream the Impossible. I used my resources like social media, networking, vendor show cases, and speaking engagements to sell my books.

Since 2015, I have released 10 books. The power of social media and the internet makes it look like those billionaires, rappers, and entrepreneurs got their success over night.

But truth be told, it took many years of waking, praying, and hard work. It's often said that success is 10 percent inspiration and 90 percent perspiration.

When pursuing your life goals, certain external obstacles may exist that prevent a person from attaining their dreams. These obstacles may include not having sufficient resources, dealing with a family crisis or struggling with an illness. However, there are times when people limit themselves as it pertains to their own success. Sometimes pursuing a dream requires a person to move out of their own way.

"Trust in the Lord with all your heart, and do not lean on your own understanding. In all your ways acknowledge him, and he will make straight your paths".

~ [Proverbs 3:5-6](#) ~

Chapter 2.
The Power Of Faith

Faith is defined as complete trust or confidence in someone or something. What is faith? Is faith real? What can we learn from the faith of others? How can we live a life of faith and encouragement that brings hope to others? Back to the original question, what is faith? Now faith is the substance of things hoped for, the evidence of things not seen.

Faith is the decision to love even when you don't feel God's presence. It is built through the decision to love, no matter the circumstances. The more you choose love, the greater your faith will grow.

Faith is the momentum of love that brings us into a peaceful future. The more faith we have, the easier it becomes to believe we can survive.

When we have no vision, our faith perishes. I think one of the biggest challenges we face is how to have faith and maintain our vision when we suffer disappointment. Prolonged disappointment makes it really easy to fall off track.

What disappointments have you experienced? Do you still talk about them? You know you're really disappointed when you stop talking about your feelings all together; the pain becomes too much, and you would rather pretend it's not there.

If you're experiencing a time of turbulence in your life, this is for you. Psalm 46:1 tells us, "God is our refuge and strength, an ever–present help in trouble."

Regardless of your circumstances, God is with you and for you. Our God is not far off.

This doesn't necessarily mean our troubles will disappear, but it does mean that God will walk with us through our trials. Like a good friend, God promises to stick with us and provide encouragement, hope and a reminder of our potential through and beyond our current situation.

Surround yourself with believers who will build you up and encourage you to fight the good fight. Sometimes all we need is a believing friend to spur us on in trusting God when the way forward may not seem clear. Allow your friends to be there and minister to you.

A Thought about Faith:

Think about your flashlight for a minute. I'll bet you haven't thought about it in a while. If you're like me, you probably aren't even sure you have one. Even if you know you have one, you may not know if it has batteries or not.

Who can blame us, really? The only time we think about flashlights is when we really need them – when we're standing in absolute darkness, wondering how we're going to get anywhere.

In this regard, the flashlight has a lot in common with **faith**, doesn't it? We often don't realize how important it is to us until the darkness and the storms come our way.

THEN we know just how important it is and we're twelve kinds of happy that we have our **faith** to call upon.

It's wise to keep a flashlight near and to make sure that it's batteries are charged and ready for service. But it's even more important to keep your faith strong by keeping your relationship with God charged and ready for service. Then, when darkness rolls in or the storms of life show up on our doorstep, we'll have the One that can truly light the way.

Chapter 3.
Dreams Bigger Than Fear

Fear is the opposite of faith. If we only trust in the things that we can see in this world, we will constantly be fearful of everything else.

You have the power to change your situation. The words you speak have more power than you think. If you continue to speak that you are broke, or never have money, you will always be that way. If you speak you are wealthy, you have money, and you are rich, you will begin to have wealth. You must have the right mindset and receive the things you put out.

Persistence is the key if you want to win. I've felt like giving up many times during my journey and the persistence to make things happen has kept me going. Understanding and truly believing that persistence delivers results will keep you moving forward.

Sometimes we forget to stop and smell the flowers. Along those lines, we also forget to celebrate the victories our efforts have created. Be proud of where you have come from and what you've achieved. Every 90 days, review the last three months, and soak up your achievements no matter how small they are.

The next time you feel like giving up, ask yourself if you've done everything possible in your current situation to maximize the opportunity.

Have you experienced all the learnings, happiness and pain associated with what you want to achieve? If the answer is no, then keep going until you have!

Be mindful of the things you place in the atmosphere.

Despite all its uncertainty, fear does make a few guarantees:

- *Fear kills dreams.*
- *Fear holds us back.*
- *Fear distorts our world.*
- *And fear determines our success or failure.*

It has the ability to infect our minds, sneak its way into our everyday language, and consume all of our thoughts —if we let it.

We can't let our fears stop us like this, if we want to achieve at the highest level. In fact, top-performers learn how to act in spite of their fears. They crush fear before it has a chance to fester and destroy.

Trust God through the process. If you want to live the life of your dreams, you must stop running from your purpose. You were created to live a life of meaning. Living your dreams can be risky, and there's always the possibility of failure. But, there's also a possibility of success.

When you stop focusing on your limiting beliefs, your fears, you are able to see a path to your dreams. Choose to live the life of your, dreams instead of the one that is limited by fear.

Chapter 4.
Fear Will Not Win

Fear, has stop me from going after my dreams. If you have faith, that means you have complete confidence or trust in something. You believe in a person or a thing without needing proof to validate your belief. For most of my life, I've felt that this is a dangerous position to put yourself in.

What is the source of fear? I think it is rooted in the assumption, that you must solve all of your problems and challenges alone. So, when I am fearful, I am also hopeless. And without hope, I find myself paralyzed. Knowing that I am not capable of changing myself or my circumstances for the better, I stand frozen.

In the past few years, however, I learned that making a living from my books, college coaching, and motivational speaking requires some degree of faith.

I believed I could make my life into what I wanted. I didn't know exactly how at the time, but I put faith in myself and believed I would figure it out.

You need to have faith in yourself. Believe that you can set out to do what you want to accomplish. Believe that you have the skills and abilities to make something great, and if you don't possess those things, believe that you're capable of developing them so you can get to work on your goals.

Fear can only win and get the best of you if you don't take action to push forward. Nothing holds people back from tapping into their full potential and becoming the best version of themselves more than fear.

It shatters dreams, prevents organizations from achieving major breakthroughs and is the root cause as to why so many end up going to their grave with all of their talents, hopes and wishes still unexpressed.

Whether you're afraid of public speaking, fear of pursuing an enormous dream, of failure or of what others may think of you, it's not actual fear that is holding you back.

It's the made-up story that you continually tell yourself about the fear that is stealing your happiness, peace of mind and the ability to unleash an unlimited amount of potential into the world.

Chapter 5.
Greatness

When the lights flicker or thunder booms, either literally or metaphorically, we have a choice. Do we choose to lean in to the fear that comes so naturally?

We can't let being afraid stop us like this if we want to achieve at the highest level. In fact, top-performers learn how to act in spite of their fears. They crush being scared before it has a chance to fester and destroy their goals.

Let's take a look at a couple of examples:
Michael Jordan

Arguably, the greatest basketball player of all time. He worked hard and overcame obstacles until he reached the pinnacle of success. He knows what it takes to overcome those barriers.

"Never say never, because limits like fears, are often just an illusion." Fears are just an illusion. Something we create in our heads that stop us from achieving at the highest level. Look where this belief got him in life: Hall of Fame, Greatest Player of All-time, and still getting multimillion-dollar endorsement deals years after playing in the NBA.

Warren Buffett

The greatest investor of our time. He's amassed so much wealth from savvy investing that he's literally bailed out entire countries on the brink of bankruptcy. Our government and top CEOs around the world turn to him in times of crises for investing advice.

Warren Buffet greatest investments have come from taking huge risks in the face of being afraid. When there's blood on the streets and nobody can think clearly about their investments, Buffett's out there buying stocks, hand over fists. He doesn't let fear stop him; in fact, he uses it to his advantage. And he's one of the wealthiest people of all time.

Milton Hershey

Hershey's is one of the most recognized names in chocolate. But before founding his company, Milton Hershey was fired from his apprenticeship with a printer. He then tried to start three different candy companies, all of which failed.

Before starting the Lancaster Caramel Company and the Hershey Company that made his sweet confection a household name.

Oprah Winfrey

Oprah Winfrey was publicly fired from her first television job as an anchor in Baltimore for getting too emotionally invested in her stories. But Winfrey rebounded and became the undisputed queen of television talk shows before amassing a media empire. Today she is worth a cool $3 billion, according to Forbes.

Madam C. J. Walker

Also known as Sarah Breedlove, Madam Walker was the first American woman to become a millionaire for her own achievements. Experiencing hair loss at an early age, she experimented with home products until she developed a workable salve.

Parlaying her $1.50-a-day job as a washer into a hair-care empire in only 12 years' time, this fascinating 19th-20th century mogul is a true inspiration and pioneer for African-Americans and businesswomen everywhere. Walker used her money to forward anti-lynching campaigns and black education.

Shawn "Jay-Z" Carter

Rap and hip-hop can't be stopped! Producing some of the most financially successful CEOs of all time, you also have to give the industry credit for producing some of the greatest stories of all time.

Another African-American born into impoverished American housing projects, Jay-Z is the current CEO of Roc Nation and his net worth is an estimated $450 million.

Chapter 6.
Believe It's Possible

Believe in yourself to know that you are worth success. Scrolling through Instagram or Facebook, it's easy to believe an idealized version of people's lives; how successful they are and how they seemingly have it all, while still being so young.

Yet, we have no idea of their real circumstances, other than the images and captions we knit together to create a idolized story. We don't know the difficult paths they had to tread to get to where they are. We have no idea of their journey, other than our perception of it.

Quick fixes, hacks and shortcuts are common in today's culture. Just like everyone else, we have fallen victim to this in the past and looked for easy ways to get ahead.

The biggest difference between successful and unsuccessful people (in health, in business, and in life) is that the ones who succeed are determined to make the situation work for them, rather than playing the role of the victim.

Believe in yourself. The biggest difference, I've noticed between successful and unsuccessful people isn't intelligence, opportunity or resources. It's the belief that they can make their goals happen.

We all deal with vulnerability, uncertainty, and failure. Some of us trust that if we move forward anyway, then we will figure it out.

When I started my business, I was the only entrepreneur in our family. There was no one for me to learn from, but I trusted that I would figure it out anyway.

Everything you have in your life is a result of your belief in yourself and the belief that it's possible. Here are the four most important steps to learning how to believe in yourself.

Practice them and you'll be amazed at the results:

- ✓ *Believe it's possible, that you can do it regardless of what anyone says or where you are in life.*
- ✓ *Visualize it. Think about exactly what your life would look like if you had already achieved your dream.*
- ✓ *Act as if. Always act in a way that is consistent with where you want to go.*
- ✓ *Take action towards your goals. Do not let fear stop you. Nothing happens in life until you take action.*

I Believe In You!

You are amazing. Take charge and incredible things can happen.

So, just imagine what next year is going to look like. And the years after that. The future is brilliantly bright, my friend.

Keep doing what you've been doing and you'll be alright. Remember there are no worst-case scenarios, because there is always a solution, a way forward. You will always survive today's challenge, so you can move on to tomorrow. Each time you overcome those challenges, you grow. You gain strength. You improve and learn and you're better for all of it.

The rest is just details. That being said, I believe in you. I believe you will have your everything a million times over.

I believe you will always take to heart those words you read as a kid, words you've read countless times again that have echoed around your head ever since: "It does not do to dwell on dreams and forget to live."

Chapter 7.

Shift Your Mindset

To help you make it to the finish line next time, here are five things you must know.

1. You must realize you are worthy of your desires. Maybe you've got a few big dreams or secret goals, but they seem a little far-fetched or somewhat out of reach. You question whether they could really happen for you. In these moments, I would urge you to ask yourself: Why not you?

So, the next time you're experiencing doubts about going after what you really want, even though your life satisfaction will suffer if you remain stuck, affirm to yourself: I choose to be great. I have what it takes.

1. Commit wholeheartedly. They say that 99% commitment is hell, but 100% commitment is golden.

2. Remember there is no such thing as failure.

3. Start wherever you are. (You have to be bad before you are good!)Many of us put off starting a new hobby, passion project, career change or dream because we're secretly scared, we'll be no good.

We're worried about failing, or worse, we'll be totally ordinary.

So, whatever it is that you're putting off, remember that if you just start today, you'll be one day closer to greatness.

Everyone always says, "Follow your dreams!" But not everyone does it.

Stay focused, go after your dreams and keep moving toward your goal.

4. Shift your mindset -- from the negativity of failure to the positivity of faith and hope. Most of our fears aren't even real. We let made-up scenarios, worries, play out in our heads and then run with them.

Over time, we really start to believe those thoughts, which more than likely are self-diminishing instead of self-empowering.

We must engrave in our minds that the only way fear can hold us back is if we let it. The only power it has is the power we give it. Shift your mind from the negative clutches of fear to the positivity of the beautiful gifts we receive when faith and hope in a bigger future are present. Then, from that point on, always look to strengthen your faith, not your fears.

Let your dreams be bigger than your fears, your actions louder than your words, and your faith stronger than your fears.

~ Author Unknown~

Chapter 8.
The journey of a thousand miles begins with a single step

You've been doing the work. You've been consistent. You've progressed. But you either hit a wall or your progress is so slow you feel like quitting altogether.

Truth be told, anyone who does anything of consequence in life feels like quitting over and over and over again.

Even though I've accomplished more than I thought possible a few years ago. I constantly feel like quitting. But I don't and I know I never will. Why? Because I know the urge to quit isn't a sign I should quit and I use the following strategies to keep pushing forward no matter what.

Focus on how far you've come: Have you seen those before and after photos of someone who's worked out for a year? The contrast between the two photos is stark. The person in the photo, however, usually doesn't realize how much they've changed until they see the comparison themselves. This analogy applies to any goal or path you've been diligently working on.

Maybe you've hit a plateau or endured some setbacks. The obstacles can become so frustrating that you figure it's time to give up on your dream. Before you abandon your mission, take some time to think about how far you've come already.

Look at how things were when you started and how they are now. Sure, you may have fallen flat a few times, but you've definitely made a great deal of progress as well. Realize the amount of strength it took you to get started in the first place and try to cultivate it again to push you towards the finish line.

Master patience: Patience is the ability to remain positive even when things aren't going your way. The person who masters patience can have everything they desire. The greatest obstacle to creativity is impatience, the almost unavoidable desire to speed up the process and make waves.

You have to constantly remind yourself that anything of great value takes diligence and consistency. Focus on the process more than the results. Even if you're making all the right moves, it may take the universe some time to catch up to your accomplishments.

The true key to effective patience stop beating yourself up throughout the entire journey. I can't tell you how many times I've needlessly beat myself up only to find my current self-wanting to tell my past self to calm down.

So I'll tell you. Calm down.
You're okay. Be patient.

When I stop to think about the alternatives of giving up on my goals and living a life of mediocrity, I simply can't bear it. The pain of those thoughts push me to keep going. In my mind, there is no choice. However, in the past, I've definitely given up on things that I once thought I wanted wholeheartedly. I didn't keep going. I simply stopped.

So what makes the difference? What's that switch in the mind that will push you past your breaking point? What's the driving force behind getting up even when you keep getting knocked down? How do you become a prized fighter who can overcome all odds to keep pushing and going even when it seemingly gets tougher and tougher to follow through

Chapter 9.
Never Give Up

As you have read, faith over fear. I challenge you to follow these ten tips.

<u>Don't be discouraged. It's often the last key in the bunch that opens the lock." Author Unknown.</u>

Never lose hope. Hope is a desire based on a promise from God. It is often said that we all need hope to survive. Hope is what dreams feed on and gets us past the tough times when life is at its worst. It is not the conviction that something will turn out well, but the certainty that something makes sense, regardless of how it turns out.

1. Make time to nurture yourself.

Hard work is important, but don't wear yourself out! You'll feel more creative, productive and satisfied if you take some time for self-care. Whether you choose to meditate, practice yoga, go for a run, have a night out or drink a glass of wine on your couch, you need to spend time taking care of your body and mind. Make sure you have your head on straight, so you can wake up every day renewed, refreshed and ready to hustle! The more you take care of yourself, the more you'll be able to take care of others.

2. Build a positive community.

Surround yourself with like-minded individuals, both in real life and online. Build a community of people who will lift you up instead of tearing you down. With a group of supportive friends, you'll have plenty of sources of ideas, inspiration and energy to help you thrive. Fill your world with positive, uplifting people, and don't leave any room for the negative ones.

3. Have a positive impact.

Be aware of how you're influencing people. Your network has their ears and eyes open, so always keep in mind the way you can impact the real world. Making others feel good is one of the best ways to boost your own happiness!

4. Get comfortable with being uncomfortable.

Don't be afraid of vulnerability. Nothing worth having comes easy. Success takes hard work and perseverance. You'll have to step outside your comfort zone, take risks and explore new possibilities to achieve your goals. You'll have to get used to a bit of struggle. Embrace it and accept it as a step on the road to success. Your hard work and discomfort will eventually pay off!

5. Learn to say 'yes' to yourself.

Seize the opportunities that come your way. If you dismiss an idea because it seems too impossible or too risky, but you still can't get it out of your head, try saying 'yes' instead.

Don't hold yourself back by playing it safe! Learn to take risks. As they say, you'll never know if you don't try. Keep yourself open to new ideas and opportunities. You never know what might happen!

6. Be authentic.

Always stay true to yourself. It's not worth pursuing a goal if you lose sight of who you are along the way. So, be unapologetically you every step of the way on your journey to achieving your dreams.

7. Know your values.

What matters to you? Family? Security? Authenticity? Your values will influence your choices and decisions and help shape your personal brand.

Do some soul-searching, and make a list of your values. Let those values guide you. Knowing your values and pursuing your true passions are vital to a happy life.

8. Set goals.

Always give yourself something to strive for. Journeys are ongoing—you'll never truly reach the end, and that's OK. When you achieve one goal, set another. Keep setting goals continuously, no matter how large or small. Knowing you have a goal to achieve will help you find the energy and motivation to keep hustling every day!

9. Don't measure your success against the success of others.

We're all our own biggest critics, but comparing yourself to someone else won't get you anywhere. Another person's success doesn't make your own success less valid. Success looks different for everyone. Celebrate your triumphs! Always strive to be the best 'you' you can be, and encourage others to be their best selves, too.

10. Never give up.

Success takes more than creativity and talent—it takes hard work, perseverance and grit. There will be bumps in the road;

the journey won't always be easy. Don't give up! Keep working, and your dreams will become realities.

Keep moving forward!

Chapter 10.
Inspiration

The truth is that the most famous people in the world have failed the most times. But they didn't stop. They didn't give up. They might have paused for a very brief period, but they kept going. Yet, they all had something that kept them moving forward. They all developed something in their hearts and their minds that pushed and pulled them towards their goals.

What's your reasons for wanting to achieve your goals? The most important thing about goal setting that you must understand is that if you don't set your goals the right way, you'll surely fail.

It's okay to feel discouraged and dissuaded at times. You're only human. But it's not okay to give up. No matter how slow you go, you have to keep going. That's how you get there. It's just one small step at a time. That's all. Just don't stop

Everyone has dreams and everyone wants to live a successful life. But it all comes down to how bad you want it. If you are willing to sacrifice the things others won't, and work like your life depends on it. You are on the right path.

It's about commitment and focus. It's about living actively instead of living passively.

Watch your thoughts, they become your words Watch your words, they become your actions Watch your actions, they become your habits Watch your habits, they become your character Watch your character, it becomes your destiny.

~ Author Unknown~

The past cannot be changed. The future is yet in your power.

~ Author Unknown~

Growth is painful.

Change is painful.

but nothing is as painful

as staying stuck somewhere

you don't belong.

~ Author Unknown~

Don't cry over the past, it's gone. Don't stress about the future, it hasn't arrived. Live in the present and make it beautiful.

~ <u>Author Unknown</u>~

Yesterday's failures are today's seeds That must be diligently planted to be able to abundantly harvest Tomorrow's success.

~ Author Unknown~

Author Bio

Born and raised in Freedmen's Town, one of that Houston Texas most important African-American historic communities, raised in a single-family household; nothing stopped Tristan Jackson from obtaining a Bachelors of Business Administration in Human Resource Management (2009) and Masters of Public Administration (2013) from Lamar University.

"I do not know the future, but one thing is for sure - God is my first priority." Ms. Jackson exclaims as she expounds on her process for writing 8 books; Dream the Impossible (2015), What to Do When Life Give You Lemons? (2016), College Success Guide (2017), I AM 30 Day Positive Affirmation(2018), Living my Best Life Journal(2018), Black Girl Magic(2018) and Faith over Fear(2019).

Currently and active College advisor for the last 10 years, Ms. Jackson is a driving force of excellence in higher education as she holds the position of Academic Advisor. "Every student I come in contact with will be aware of every opportunity and every resource available to them to attend college."

She affirms while obtaining yet another Doctoral Degree from Texas Southern University in Educational Administration completion date slated for 2021.

In addition to serving as a mentor, Ms. Jackson is active in her community through hosting events such as, Back to School Prayer Care of Love (toiletry drive for seniors), Pre-Mother's Day Dinner and College 101 Prep Events.

Tristan Jackson invites you to personally connect with her on her website, www.tjinspires.com and follow her on these social platforms: Instagram, YouTube, and Facebook.

JOURNAL

Made in the USA
Middletown, DE
22 February 2019